YOUR KNOWLEDGE

- We will publish your bachelor's and master's thesis, essays and papers

- Your own eBook and book - sold worldwide in all relevant shops

- Earn money with each sale

Upload your text at www.GRIN.com and publish for free

E. Dimant, M. Dysart, K. Lanoix, T. Leung, S. Lindner

Prêt A Manger. A Business Model Analysis

GRIN Publishing

Bibliographic information published by the German National Library:

The German National Library lists this publication in the National Bibliography; detailed bibliographic data are available on the Internet at http://dnb.dnb.de .

This book is copyright material and must not be copied, reproduced, transferred, distributed, leased, licensed or publicly performed or used in any way except as specifically permitted in writing by the publishers, as allowed under the terms and conditions under which it was purchased or as strictly permitted by applicable copyright law. Any unauthorized distribution or use of this text may be a direct infringement of the author s and publisher s rights and those responsible may be liable in law accordingly.

Imprint:

Copyright © 2010 GRIN Verlag GmbH
Print and binding: Books on Demand GmbH, Norderstedt Germany
ISBN: 978-3-640-82026-9

This book at GRIN:

http://www.grin.com/en/e-book/165865/pret-a-manger-a-business-model-analysis

GRIN - Your knowledge has value

Since its foundation in 1998, GRIN has specialized in publishing academic texts by students, college teachers and other academics as e-book and printed book. The website www.grin.com is an ideal platform for presenting term papers, final papers, scientific essays, dissertations and specialist books.

Visit us on the internet:

http://www.grin.com/

http://www.facebook.com/grincom

http://www.twitter.com/grin_com

Coverbild: Pinkyone @Shutterstock.com; Freepik.com

Table of Contents

1.0 Overview 2

2.0 Business Model 2

    2.1 Segmentation 2

    2.2 Screening and Corporate Social Responsibility 3

    2.3 Growth Strategy 4

3.0 Canadian Market 4

    3.1 Canadian Eating Habits 4

    3.2 Canadian Competitors 5

    3.3 Prêt's Core Values in Canada.. 5

4.0 Options 6

    4.1 Toronto, Ontario 6

    4.2 Montréal, Québec 7

    4.3 Vancouver, British Columbia.. 7

5.0 Recommendation 8

    5.1 Assumptions 8

    5.2 Final Recommendation 8

6.0 Implementation 9

    6.1 Location.. 9

    6.2 Recruitement 9

    6.3 Marketing 10

    6.4 Suppliers... 11

    6.5 Adaptation to Canadian market... 11

7.0 Future Outlook... 12

Appendix 13

Bibliography 16

1.0 Overview

A passion for food was the driving force for Sinclair Beecham and Julian Metcalfe, two college friends who were hungry for tasty and healthy sandwiches, when they opened the first Prêt a Manger in 1986. The company was founded in London, England on the basis of making proper sandwiches while avoiding obscure chemicals, additives and preservatives that were common for prepared food in the market at the time.[1] This one of a kind restaurant blossomed, as it offered consumers a product that could not found anywhere else.[2] Prêt a Manger has differentiated itself in three main categories: the menu, the level of customer service and the dedication to sustainability. A soup, sandwich or salad from Prêt a Manger is made with all natural ingredients. There are no artificial colours or no additives, just good taste. They get their supplies from local vendors and are always looking for new flavours in the area.[3] Poor service cannot be found in a Prêt a Manger store. The staff are all exceptionally trained and treated for the best overall customer experience. Prêt a Manger's sustainability goals, which are primarily to reduce their environmental impact, are updated regularly as they want to continuously decrease their environmental footprint. The food industry leaves a lot of room for waste, but not for Prêt a Manger. They donate all their unsold sandwiches, salads and baguettes to the homeless at the end of each day. Prêt a Manger is privately owned, and thus does not have the pressure to grow as quickly as a public company does.[4] However, they are continuously growing. There are over 200 stores in the UK and Prêt a Manger has expanded to New York City, Chicago, Washington DC and Hong Kong. Prêt a Manger is synonymous with good taste.

2.0 Business Model

Prêt a Manger's underlying value proposition is to serve great-tasting freshly made sandwiches with a business model that is dedicated to social responsibility. Prêt a Manger offers a wide selection of products with over 200 sandwiches, salads and soups of highest quality. Therefore, not only does the quality play an important role, but so does the commitment to a comprehensive service. A 2010 London survey, conducted among immigrants in the company, founds that Prêt a Manger was the most desirable place to work. Consequently, Prêt a Manger "won the 2010 award for best retail company in the UK. The company earned this award through a commitment to its people and to its fresh preservative free food."[5] While combining sophisticated service with high-quality food, the company tries to maintain their three core-merits throughout their value chain: "First and foremost, we are passionate about food and keeping it fresh and interesting. This is our core product and we work hard to produce the best we can [...]. The second Prêt a Manger passion is their staff, all 2,200 of them spread across 116 stores (25 outside London) in the UK [...]. The third and final part of Prêt a Manger's sandwich success story is to be passionate and proud of the business and what they have achieved."[6]

2.1 Segmentation

Unlike their direct competition (e.g. Subway), the company is aiming for a high-price-high-quality segment. "Its French name and comparatively adventurous menu all helped create an aura of exclusivity - instead of ham and tomato sandwiches, Prêt a Manger offered Brie, tomato and basil baguettes."[7] As this is especially the case for their main business in London "at

£1.20 for a tiny bottle of orange juice, it is targeting urban professionals with little time on their hands."[8] The commitment to sophisticated service can also be experienced by the service speed. "Customers spend just 90 seconds from the time they get in line to the time they leave the shop."[9] Although Prêt a Manger never truly engaged in extensive market research, the mix of delightful and more expensive sandwiches with low-priced products, like their 99 cents coffee, reveals the company's ambivalent business model, which applies to heterogeneous needs of their equally heterogeneous clientele. "We like to maximize the space we have in our shops and use this to help promote our food. We use large "gilt frames" which sit in our windows. These help spread the message of our seasonal product launches."[10] By that, Prêt a Manger was profiled as "an excellent example of an organization that creates a unique experience for a clearly targeted group of customers and delivers value everyday through its people and products. It has good processes and customer friendly policies. What Prêt a Manger does not do is advertise, but there is little need to do this because its customers promote the organization."[11] This clearly emphasizes the fact that the company is able to successfully adapt their business model to their customers' needs. The great challenge for each company is to match their own perceptions and expectations about how to create sustainable value with the customer's perceived value recognition. In the 2001 Forum Survey a great volatility in both, companies' and customers' value acknowledgment, was identified (**Appendix A**)[12]

There are often perception differences between customers and companies in the features and response to problems. To ensure a feasible convergence of both, the company established a close interaction with their consumers through communication channels, anticipating that 19 out of 20 unsatisfied customers would rather leave the store quietly than voice their complaint.[13]

"On average, 60 per cent of feedback received by the Prêt a Manger customer service department is either positive or neutral."[14] The emphasis on high-quality service is no coincidence. As discovered in a survey, "Customers who rate you a five on a scale from one (poor) to five (excellent) are six times more likely to buy from you again, compared to those who rate you a four on the same scale. The economic benefits of retaining repeat customers and building repeat business are compelling."[15] The people make the difference and retaining customers by satisfying their needs not only saves costs, as attracting new customers can generate three to ten times higher costs than holding old clientele, but it also impacts the company's outward perception through customer's loyalty and positive word-of-mouth marketing, intrinsically generated by the very same satisfied people.[16]

2.2 Screening and Corporate Social Responsibility

To maintain a high level of quality in their personnel, the company implemented an attentive screening procedure to screen their job applicants. "There is a rigorous assessment for each potential employee. We make them work in a shop for a few days, they have several interviews and, in each case, we try to get to know them as individuals."[17] As a result, the company has become very passionate about their staff and the types of individuals they hire. The company believes that they are an important part of the company's culture and has always been eager to treat them exceedingly well. The company does not only incorporate their voice in business matters, but also pays them fair salary and wage for their hard to keep them continuously motivated.[18]

The company's attitude to engage in corporate social responsibility is becoming apparent in how they treat their employees' and in their solicitousness towards fresh food. All of their

3

offered menu dishes are completely free from any preservatives and consist solely of natural ingredients. In addition, the daily-prepared sandwiches are not stored overnight, but are given away to charities if they are not sold that day.[19]

2.3 Growth Strategy

Prêt a Manger's did not just start their business in London because both founders, Sinclair Beecham and Julian Metcalfe, graduated at the Polytechnic of Central London, but did so because they were driven by a growing resentment towards the regularly served "soggy sandwiches and mush for lunch, often served with a snarl, from local sandwich shops."[20] With having found this untapped market niche, they decided to step in and fill the gap with a business that was committed to serving high-quality food. Starting their business in Victoria, the company has successfully established over 200 stores worldwide to date.[21] The company's understanding of growth is research based and the company tries to incorporate as many business impacting variables as possible into their business model. "When positioning on a busy high street, we need to make sure we cater for the range and diversity of people who may enter one of our shops. We therefore have a large range of food products to suit different tastes."[22]

With the intention of accomplishing oversees business growth, the company has become well aware that it is important to have an experienced backup-partner. "It is this transatlantic venture which has led to McDonald's involvement – the two founders realized that if they wanted to sell their concept in another country, they needed heavyweight backing."[23] This would allow the company to concentrate on their business while benefiting from McDonalds' big expertise in overseas business adaptation.

Having the company's core values and business perceptions in mind, this model proves to be successful on many levels. Through the combination of customer satisfaction, high-quality food and sustainable business growth, the company is becoming a global success. "The Prêt employment system works because at the end of the day their employees like working at Prêt and are rewarded for performing at, or above, Prêt a Manger's expectations. The result: customers get great product and service and not only stay, but over time become fiercely loyal."[24]

3.0 Canadian Market

Canada's service sector has grown rapidly over the last few years, especially when compared to other sectors in the Canadian economy. The economy's GDP, once dependent on agriculture and mining, is now generated by banks, consulting firms and health care assistance. Accommodation and food services are among those sub sectors with the highest growth rates.[25]

Prêt a Manger is currently doing business in three countries. To evaluate whether Prêt a Manger should enter the Canadian market, it should determine if the Canadian market shares similar characteristics with Prêt a Manger's existing markets. Only if Prêt a Manger's values coincide with societal or cultural factors in Canada, will the expansion to Canada be successful. In the following, Canadian eating and lifestyle habits will be examined.

3.1 Canadian Eating Habits

Prêt a Manger's products are all take-away products. Although most restaurants have seating areas, their products are designed to be convenient to eat while on the run. Thus, Prêt a

Manger primarily targets consumers who want to have a quick meal. A study on Canadian Food Trends showed that Canadians opted more often for convenient snacks throughout the day rather than having a traditional, time-consuming lunch. Portable food in general and sandwiches in particular, have gained popularity as they are a quick and reasonably-priced alternative to eating in restaurants.[26]

Families' lifestyles have become busier as the participation of women in Canada's workforce continues to rise. Ready-to-eat food options are used to cut down food preparation time.[27] A survey among Canadians showed that the percentage of persons who consume something prepared in a fast-food outlet are highest among consumer aged 14 to 50 years of age, with the highest figure among men between 19 and 30 years.[28]

Attributable to government initiatives, public awareness for diet and related health issues in the Canadian society is continuously growing. Consumers are increasingly giving their attention to health issues which are linked to diet and lifestyle, such as diabetes, high cholesterol or cardiovascular diseases. Overall, nutritional concerns are more important to women. They tend to seek more information concerning nutritional value and make more selective food choices. The result of the new health consciousness Canadians, can be seen in the decline of fat consumption. The sales of soft drink and snack food are also experiencing a downward trend. However, certain circumstances are perceived to impede healthy eating. Lack of time, confusion regarding nutritional labels or scepticism of actual healthiness of food products are among the main obstacles for consumers' healthy nutrition.[29]

Prêt a Manger strives to eliminate all these concerns and barriers. They offer a diversity of sandwiches that are ready-to-eat and healthy at the same time. In addition, a nutritional breakdown of each product is available, both online and in the shops.[30]

3.2 Canadian Competitors

Prêt a Manger's competitors include those who sell fresh sandwiches and that offer a fast and easy meal. Prêt a Manger's main competitors are Subway, Tim Hortons, Quizno's Sandwiches, Mr. Sub, and certain fast-food chains that are adding more nutritious choices, like healthy sandwiches, to their menus.[31] Prêt a Manger will not only need to compete with the well known restaurant but will also compete with smaller neighbourhood sandwich shops. As Prêt a Manger also offers complimentary products to their sandwiches, such as soups or salads, it could be concluded that any restaurant could be an indirect competitor. However, Prêt a Manger's unique value proposition of high-quality freshly made products will help differentiate the company from their competitors in the Canadian market.

3.3 Prêt a Manger's Core Values in Canada

Canadian consumers are becoming more conscious of safety and quality where food is concerned. Canadians continue to worry about animal diseases (avian influenza, BSE, etc.), try to avoid food additives and preservatives and pay attention to processing techniques. Organic foods are increasingly becoming more popular; the organic foods market is growing at an estimated rate of about 15 to 20 per cent per year. As more and more outlets offer organic food, it is becoming a mainstream product. Moreover, quality is often being equated with freshness, taste and naturalness.[32] All these trends go with Prêt a Manger's core values, which include shunning all food additives and purchasing regional foods whenever possible.[33]

Prêt a Manger is also committed to high animal welfare for its meat and dairy products. This will be appreciated by Canadian customers, as the ethical treatment of animals is likely to become a more topical issue in the Canadian media. Moreover, Canadians tend to pay more attention to the traceability of the country of origin when it comes to food products. This is for safety reasons (to reduce food contamination) as well as for social and economic reasons. Consumers might opt to avoid food from countries where environmental or labour standards are not met. On the other hand, fair-trade and local products might be supported.[34] Prêt a Manger ensures that their ingredients come from local and sustainable sources wherever possible and provides extensive data on the countries of origin of all of their ingredients.[35]

4.0 Options

When determining the location of the new Prêt a Manger, it is important to conduct an analysis on Canadian cities to see which would fit the Prêt a Manger's business model. According to their business model, it is important for the restaurant to be located in an area where they can access fresh local products in a well established agriculture market. In addition, consumers must also be willing to purchase a premium quality product at a premium price. Finally, the potential for growth within the area is a key factor in determining future stability of the restaurant. As a result, Prêt a Manger has targeted many metropolitan cities when entering a new country (ex. New York City in the U.S). Based on these aspects, it is believed that Prêt a Manger should consider three of Canada's largest metropolitan cities: Toronto, Vancouver and Montreal. All three cities have certain characteristics that would make them a good choice for Prêt a Manger to locate their restaurant. Toronto is usually seen as an economic power, while Vancouver has beautiful scenery and a high amount of tourism and Montreal is a culturally diverse city. An analysis on these three cities was conducted to determine whether they are a viable option for a new Prêt a Manger.

4.1 Toronto, Ontario

Toronto is one of the most multicultural cities in the world.[36] It has a population of 2.48 million people and a population of 5.5 million people in the Greater Toronto Area.[37] From the 2006 Census, 28 per cent of ethnic origin responses in Toronto were from European descent, with 19 per cent coming from the British Isles (England, Scotland, and Ireland); 16 per cent were East or Southeast Asian; and 10 per cent were South Asian.[38] In addition, 56.2 per cent of the population speaks English, while 1.4 per cent of the population speaks French.[39]

The Food and Beverage industry are one of the top ten industries in Toronto.[40] The city is built on, and is next to some of Canada's best agricultural land.[41] It also has a high concentration of value-added food processors.[42] This would provide Prêt a Manger with excellent access to fresh products needed to make their sandwiches and other goods. In addition, many Torontonians increasingly understand that food is connected with health, the environment, the economy and community.[43] Consequently, there has been a growing interest in home cooking, farmers' markets, specialty food stores, food entrepreneurship, volunteering with neighbourhood food projects, learning about nutrition, and supporting local farms and healthy and sustainable food.[44] It has been found that food prices in Toronto food prices are slightly lower than Vancouver, but much higher than Montreal.[45] In 2008, the average household in Toronto spent $8,132 on food.[46] As Toronto is one of the major food cities in the world, there are over 4,000 food retail outlets and over 6,000 restaurants that represent more than 200 different food cultures.[47] Furthermore, the Ontario government recently amended regulations to allow street vendors to sell a broader range of foods.[48]

In 2006, the average annual income of a Torontonian household was $80,343, for families $96,602, for non family persons $39,068.[49] During the economic recession in 2009, Toronto's total employment declined by 1.4 per cent.[50] The number of full-time employees fell by 17,500 to 1,006,400 and the number of part-time employees fell by 600 to 284,800.[51] However, the Canadian economy is beginning to recover from the recession and statistics show that consumer confidence in Ontario is on the rise.[52] Furthermore, Toronto is beginning to implement a growth management strategy for its downtown core.[53] This plan will involve a diverse mix of employment growth and residential growth, making Downtown Toronto a popular place to live, work, and do business.[54]

4.2 Montréal, Québec

Montreal is consistently rated as one of the world's most "liveable" cities, and was called "Canada's Cultural Capital" by Monocle Magazine.[55] Today, Montreal has a population of 1.6 million people.[56] The city has one of the most culturally diverse populations in Canada where one out of three people are born outside the country.[57] The most prominent cultures include Chinese, Italian and Haitian.[58] There are also large clusters of people from European ethnicity, such as the French, British and Irish.[59] According to the Charter of the French Language, the official labour language in Québec is French.[60] This could present a challenge for a Prêt a Manger as the company will need consider how they may overcome the communication barrier if they were to open a Prêt a Manger in Montreal.

Montreal has some of the finest restaurants and bars in North America.[61] However, Montreal food consumption trends showed that consumers were the least concerned with nutrition when compared to Canadians across Canada.[62] This may present a problem for Prêt a Manger as their strategy is focused on providing healthy and nutritious food options. In addition, Statistics Canada found that the average household spent $7,568 on food in 2008, and this represented 17 per cent of total current consumption in the city of Montreal.[63]

"Montreal's economy is the second largest of all cities in Canada based on GDP."[64] The average income for a household in Montreal is $33,000 and 65 per cent of the population are active in the work-force.[65] In addition, Montreal has a "world-class" agri-food industry including more than 45,000 employees.[66]

4.3 Vancouver, British Columbia

Vancouver is the eighth largest city in Canada, and the third largest metropolitan area with a population of 2.1 million.[67] It has a strong multicultural basis, with the percentage of citizens whose first language is English at 49.1 per cent and citizens whose first language is Chinese at 25.3 per cent.[68] Furthermore, it is not surprising that Vancouver's population continues to grow as it has repeatedly been named the most liveable city in the world.[69] This assessment was based on stability, healthcare, culture and environment, education and infrastructure.

Vancouver is currently enjoying one of the strongest economic expansions in years. The strength of Greater Vancouver has propelled the province to continue to outperform the national benchmark.[70] Among other factors, the competitive business and tax climate make it an ideal place to open a new business. When comparing Vancouver to other major Western cities in North America such as Seattle, San Diego, San Jose and Las Vegas; Vancouver has a much lower cost of doing business.[71] As can be seen in **Appendix** B, the median annual income of Vancouver is higher than that of Canada and Montreal, but slightly lower than Toronto[72].

Vancouver residents are healthy consumers, with farmer's markets enjoying 30 to 35 per cent annual growth.[73] It has become even more evident that the majority of residents are willing to pay a premium for local products.[74] Its dedication to local products is another step in the "green" direction for Vancouver. The city currently has initiatives for sustainability, with the current Mayor having launched the Greenest City initiative in 2009, with the goal of being the greenest city by 2020[75]. Prêt a Manger's business model fits well within the Vancouver atmosphere. Vancouver could also benefit from Prêt a Manger's entrance as homelessness has been growing at an alarming rate since 2002.[76] Vancouver as a whole, is extremely comparable to the U.K. from a business and consumer standpoint. As a result, Prêt a Manger would have an ideal location here.

5.0 Recommendation

5.1 Assumptions

It is assumed that Prêt a Manger is aware of the costs of opening a store in Canada and has the finances to fund its expansion. It is also assumed that Prêt a Manger will have one of its Field Experts or a Project Manager to help enter the Canadian market. These individuals would have the experience in helping set-up a Prêt a Manger in a foreign country. In addition, they are very familiar with all Prêt a Manger's culture and procedures. To assist with the legal logistics of opening a store in the Canadian market, Prêt a Manger would hire a lawyer who is well versed in Canadian business law to ensure that Prêt a Manger is following all the right procedures in accordance with Canadian and Ontario laws and regulations.

5.2 Final Recommendation

After analyzing these options, it is recommended that Prêt a Manger enter the Canadian market by setting up a store in Toronto's Financial District. It has been found that the Canadian market is similar to the UK market and exhibits Prêt a Manger's values; therefore their expansion to Canada will likely be successful. Prêt will be entering the Canadian market independently as it fits their current expansion model of expanding organically and independently.[77] Furthermore, the company is opposed to franchising their business because they want to have continued control over their brand name and brand image.[78] As a private company, they maintain the right to operate their company the way they see fit which allows them to maintain of high-quality customer service, products, and employees. Toronto has many advantages when compared to Montreal and Vancouver because it has a larger population, thus providing Prêt the opportunity to grow in the future by opening more stores in the city. English is the primary language spoken in the city; therefore Prêt will not have to worry about the language barriers which may include having to hire a bilingual staff or having to redesign they're packaging to have both English and French descriptions. If Prêt wants to make its mark in the Canadian market, Toronto is the place to do this because the Food and Beverage industry is one of Toronto's top ten industries. In addition, Prêt would have access to an abundance of fresh products to make their. Over the last few years, there has been an increasing trend to be more health conscious in choice of food selection. Prêt would be able to capitalize on this opportunity by providing customers with healthy choices of fruit salads, fresh fruit, a variety of sandwiches, baguettes and more. Lastly, as Canada's economic capital, the average household in Toronto makes more than those in Montreal and Vancouver. Therefore, they are capable to purchase a premium good for their health conscious need.

6.0 Implementation

6.1 Location

The location chosen for the Prêt a Manger store is on the corner of Adelaide St. W and Sheppard St. which is in the centre of the Financial District. See **Appendices C and D** for further details of the location. It was determined that this was the ideal location because the store would be centered in a high traffic area during its operating hours. Therefore, there will be an abundance of business people looking for a healthy (as opposed to unhealthy choices) and new lunch alternative that they can get quickly without having to wait in line for a long period of time. Prêt a Manger will offer a healthy choice to meet these consumers' needs. The location faces an entrance to First Canadian Place, a downtown shopping mall, which will increase traffic and visibility of the store. The location is approximately 1,035 square feet and outdoor space that could be dedicated to a seating area. [79] It is a corner unit with ample window space. It is assumed that since a Tim Horton's has already resided there that there it has the space for a kitchen.

Competition for this location is similar to that which they would face in London. There is a variety of small fast food places such as sushi, pizza and cafes. Their main competition in this area would be Subway or Tim Horton's as both of these companies carry fresh sandwiches. However, the competition is solely based on the production of sandwiches as Prêt a Manger provides a healthy alternative to the regular fast food menu.

6.2 Recruitment

To staff the new Prêt a Manger location, Prêt a Manger will outsource its staffing and recruitment procedures to AFFINITY Resource Management Inc. Prêt a Manger will outsource this because the company does not have access to its human resource personnel in London to conduct the procedures themselves. AFFINITY is a Toronto based human resource consulting firm that is well known for their ability to provide human resource solutions for each firm's specific needs and goals.[80] Their staff will work closely with the Project Manager at Prêt a Manger to ensure that the company's needs are all met, on time and on budget. Prêt a Manger will need to outline the KSAOs (knowledge, skills, abilities, and other characteristics) and job requirements the staff and store manager will need to possess for their positions. In the past, Prêt has focused on finding employees who possess a *passion* in the work they do, are able to *clearly talk*, and is able to *work well on a team*. An outline of what Prêt a Manger wants to see in their team, what they don't want to see, and what is considered to be Prêt Perfect is in **Appendix E**. This guideline will help AFFINITY to develop job advertisements for the positions available.

9

AFFINITY will help Prêt a Manger determine the best places to advertise their jobs in order to have a wider selection of qualified applicants to apply for the position. Prêt likes to ensure that its employees are happy by compensating them for their hard work, rather than as little as they can get away with.[81] The company usually provides an hourly wage and salary (General Managers) that is slightly higher than minimum wage to keep their employees happy.[82] Currently, Prêt offers stakeholder's pensions; health insurance; reimbursements eye tests; flexible working arrangements offered on an ad hoc basis; 28 days of holidays for full-time staff; incentive pay and performance-related pay; and fifty per cent discounts for employees, friends, and families on all foods and drinks at the company.[83] The Project Manager will work with AFFINITY to ensure that the wage and benefits given to Canadian employees follows Canadian laws, regulations and norms, within Prêt a Manger's budget, and follows the Prêt a Manger philosophy of employee treatment. AFFINITY will screen applicants that have applied for positions at Prêt and set-up and interview potential employees for them.

Each Prêt shop has trainers within their core staff.[84] However, much of employee training takes place at Prêt a Manger's Training Academy in Victoria, England where employees are taught to attain the expected level of customer service, the procedures to ordering and maintaining ingredients, and more.[85] As it would be costly to send all Canadian employees to this Academy, Prêt a Manger will need to have two or more of its trainers come to Toronto to train the employees at the store or in the local area. This will be more cost effective than sending Canadian employees to Victoria, England.

6.3 Marketing

When entering a new market, a company will always need to market the product, especially if it is in a new country. Prêt a Manger must be prepared to market its product to the new consumers in Toronto. Since the restaurant will be established in the Financial District, it is likely that many business individuals will already know of the restaurant if they may have traveled to any of the cities that Prêt a Manger has already established its stores and brand name. However, it is also important to promote its brand and products to new potential customers. According to Prêt a Manger's Customer Services Manager, the company keeps its direct marketing down to a minimum.[86] Instead the company relies on its value proposition, which is to satisfy customers, and this in turn leads to viral word-of-mouth marketing. Furthermore, Prêt a Manger practices relationship marketing which means that the company believes that investing in staff and high-quality ingredients, will be a more effective means of promotion due to positive word of mouth, which builds strong relationships with their customers.[87] However, to be able to promote the product to new potential customers the store in Toronto will be using banners and posters in their restaurant, and there will also be small billboards placed in the Financial District. These small billboards will be placed in highly visible areas to help attract a higher number of customers to the store. It is expected that these billboards will be placed one month before the store opens, to raise awareness about the new opening of Prêt a Manger, and one month after the opening to keep the Prêt a Manger name in people's minds when deciding where to have their lunch. Once the Prêt a Manger's name is in the consumers' minds, it will increase the probability of having these consumers come to Prêt a Manger for lunch more often as regular customers. As Prêt a Manger grows in Toronto, the company will look at whether the company will need to expand their marketing without moving too far from the company's business model.

6.4 Suppliers

Another important step for Prêt a Manger to consider when opening a store in Toronto is to find adequate suppliers that can provide fresh ingredients for its products. As mentioned earlier, Toronto is surrounded by agricultural land with a high density of farms, and food processors can be found all over the Toronto area. This is convenient for Prêt a Manger, as purchasing locally means that the company can meet their goal of having a sustainable supply chain.

One of Prêt a Manger's key ingredients for their sandwiches is bread. Customers can choose between whole-grain and 7-grain bloomer bread.[88] A certified organic bakery that would meet the company's expectations is the Bäckerhaus Veit in Woodbridge, Ontario.[89] Alternatively, they could source organic bread and pastries from the Kensington Natural Bakery, which produces these items a few kilometres away from Prêt a Manger's store in Downtown Toronto.[90] With regards to meat, Prêt a Manger could either cooperate with individual farmers or opt to source from a wholesaler such as "The Healthy Butcher" in Toronto. "The Healthy Butcher" provides a variety of meat products from local organic farmers.[91] Eggs, cheese and other dairy products can be purchased from the "Organic Meadow" farm in Guelph, Ontario.[92] Certified organic vegetables and fruit could be provided by the "Plan B Organic Farm", located in Branchton, Ontario.[93] This farm is about 100 kilometers distance to Toronto, the transportation of goods from this location might not be the most eco-friendly delivery. However, since the farm grows much of Prêt a Manger's required ingredients; it is a convenient alternative to having several smaller suppliers who can substitute a combination of shorter distance deliveries.

Once Prêt a Manger has decided on the suppliers who will supply their ingredients, the company will need to specify the delivery details, such as time, frequency and mode of transportation. Similar to their existing stores, Prêt a Manger is likely to arrange for daily early morning deliveries so the ingredients can be fresh when production starts. Some products might not be able to be sourced locally. In this situation, Prêt a Manger should try to coordinate delivery with its other shops in North America in order to keep delivery costs and the environmental burden at a minimum. So far, Basil is the only one of Prêt a Manger's ingredients to be air-freighted, while all others are transported land-based.[94]

Since Prêt a Manger sells products from the same date only, the store will have a considerable amount of unsold food left at the end of every business day. Similar to their operations in other cities, Prêt a Manger will offer it to local charities, such as the "Good Shepherd Ministries," "The Yonge Street Mission" or the "Fort York Food Bank". [95]

6.5 Adaptation to Canadian market

In order to successfully enter the Canadian market Prêt a Manger needs to perform a proper change management. Even though Canada has a direct proximity to the US, where Prêt a Manger has already gained experience by joining that market in 2000, the circumstances in Canada are somewhat different. Having the unsuccessful initial move to New York in mind, Prêt a Manger has to do things differently right from the start. Every market environment is heterogeneous and is unique; therefore, Prêt a Manger will need to adapt to the Canadian market's tastes, customers, and value expectations. Transferring the same business model from one country to another might not work well. This was proven to be the case when Prêt a Manger first joined the U.S. market.

To outperform their own expectations, the company needs to adapt to the Canadian market in various ways, which may include adjusting their menu to local tastes. Having in mind that Prêt a Manger is not as well known in Canada as it is in the UK, the company should avoid overwhelming the customers with a tremendous repertoire of sandwiches. Initially, Prêt a Manger should focus selling 30 of their most popular sandwiches, with the addition of some new Canadian specific sandwich creations (e.g. incorporating Maple Syrup). In addition, the company needs to focus more heavily on healthy food options to seize the market when they first enter, as this goes hand in hand with the growing nutrition awareness of the Canadians and Prêt a Manger's values.

7.0 Future Outlook

Prêt a Manger has a successful business model that taps into a market niche where consumers are nutrition-aware individuals looking for high-quality food that is freshly-made. Therefore, the company is ready to make its move into the Canadian market. By having performed a thorough market screening, competitors' analysis, change management and local adaptation, the question is not whether, but to what extent Prêt a Manger is going to successfully diversify its portfolio by expanding into the Canadian market. Having no real competitors to face, the company will be able to create a strong and positive brand awareness. This will autonomously drive up the demand for Prêt a Manger's range of products and will help spread the Prêt a Manger's message virally. After having effectively captured a magnificent market share in Toronto, the company needs to remain open-minded with regard to further growth in the city and in other geographic locations. This will ensure proximity to potential customers and Prêt a Manger's ability reach a wider customer base, which is a great market and business opportunity in such a big country and shouldn't be disregarded.

Appendices

Appendix A

Appendix B

Table 1. Median Household Income for Select Metropolitan Areas, 2001 - 2006

Geographic Area	Median Household Income (2001)	Median Household Income (2006)	Change in Median Household Income (2001 - 2006) $	%
Canada	46,752	53,634	6,882	15%
Vancouver CMA	49,940	55,231	5,291	11%
Toronto CMA	59,502	64,128	4,626	8%
Montreal CMA	42,123	47,979	5,856	14%
Calgary CMA	58,861	68,579	9,718	17%
Edmonton CMA	51,685	63,082	11,397	22%
Victoria CMA	46,387	53,310	6,923	15%

Source: Statistics Canada, 2001, 2006 Census

Source: http://www.metrovancouver.org/about/publications/Publications/Bulletin_12_final_June2009.pdf

Appendix C

Appendix D

Appendix E

✦ Passion ✦
Pace, pride, ownership, resilience, high standards

DON'T WANT TO SEE	WANT TO SEE	PRET PERFECT!
	Is enthusiastic	
Needs close management	Has initiative. Doesn't wait to be told	Role model
Blames others	Wants Pret to be the best	Never gives up
Becomes flustered when the heat is on	Takes ownership for their work	Always does their best
Does things only for show	Cares about standards	Admits their mistakes
Is just here for the money	Works at pace	Loves food
	Copes well with pressure	Goes the extra mile

✦ Clear talking ✦
Straightforward, clear, informal, thoughtful, interesting, sensitive

DON'T WANT TO SEE	WANT TO SEE	PRET PERFECT!
Uses jargon inappropriately	Communicates sensitively	
Over complicates ideas	Listens	Communication with conviction
Confuses people	Is sincere	Paints a clear picture
Is complacent about the business	Admits when they don't understand or makes mistakes	Constructively disagrees
Agrees blandly with others	Express ideas concisely	Communicates upwards honestly
Minces words	Uses an informal style	Knows their audience
Over relies on email		

✦ Team working ✦
Fun, caring, sociable, quirky, helpful

DON'T WANT TO SEE	WANT TO SEE	PRET PERFECT!
		Anticipates others' needs
Moody or bad tempered	Creates a sense of fun	Goes out of their way to be helpful
Doesn't interact with others	Is genuinely friendly	Is charming to people
Thinks only about their own needs	Is happy to be themself	Sets the tone for the group
Annoys people	Helps others	Cares about other people's happiness
Is intolerant of others	Respects others	Has presence

Bibliography

600 to 800 square feet Downtown East and Financial Core Toronto
http://officesearchtoronto.com/2010/01/20/600-to-800-square-feet-dowtown-east-and-financial-core-toronto/ (30 November 2010).

"2006 Census Highlights," *Ministry of Finance*,
<http://www.fin.gov.on.ca/en/economy/demographics/census/cenhi06-8.pdf> (30 November 2010).

Agri-food – General Industry Profile, *Montreal International*, 2009
http://www.montrealinternational.com/en/invest/sectors/agri-food.html (28 November 2010)

"About Montreal", *Mines Without Borders – CIM*, 2010
http://www.cim.org/montreal2011/registration/Montreal.cfm (28 November 2010)

"About our Company" *Pret A Manger*, 2010
http://www.pret.com/us/about_our_company/good_natural_food/ (29 November 2010).

"About Us" *Pret A Manger*, 2010 http://www.pret.com/about/ (29 November 2010).

About Vancouver, *City of Vancouver* 2010 http://vancouver.ca/aboutvan.htm (29 November 2010).

"A Wealth of Food: A Profile of Toronto's Food Economy," *Toronto Food Policy Council*, January 1999, http://www.toronto.ca/health/tfpc_wealth.pdf (27 November 2010).

"Average household expenditures, by selected metropolitan area – Ottawa-Gatineau, Toronto," *Statistics Canada*, 2008, http://www40.statcan.gc.ca/l01/cst01/famil10d-eng.htm (28 November 2010).

Average household expenditures, by selected metropolitan area -Québec, Montréal", *Statistics Canada*, 2008 http://www40.statcan.ca/l01/cst01/famil10c-eng.htm (28 November 2010)

Bäckerhaus Veit, no date, http://www.backerhausveit.com/index.php (28 November 2010).

Backgrounder on the City of Vancouver Low-Income Housing Survey and Pivot Legal Society, *Pivot Legal Society*, 2005, http://intraspec.ca/Vancouver_Low-IncomeHousingSurvey2005.pdf (29 November 2010).

Canadians' Eating Habits", p. 25, *Statistics Canada,* May 2007, http://www.statcan.gc.ca/pub/82-003-x/2006004/article/habit/9609-eng.pdf (26 November 2010).

"Canadian Food Trends to 2020", p. 25-26, *Agriculture and Agri-Food Canada Ontario*, July 2005, http://www4.agr.gc.ca/resources/prod/doc/agr/pdf/ft-ta_eng.pdf (26 November 2010).

Chrissy Aitchison, "Toronto Soup Kitchens and Food Banks", 12 December 2009, http://www.blogto.com/city/2009/12/toronto_soup_kitchens_and_food_banks/ (28 November 2010).

"Consumer confidence improving: Conf. Board," *CBC News*, 24 November 2010, http://www.cbc.ca/canada/toronto/story/2010/11/24/consumer-confidence-holiday-shopping.html?ref=rss (28 November 2010).

Economic Profile, *Vancouver Economic Development Comission,* 2010, http://www.vancouvereconomic.com/page/economic-profile (29 November 2010).

"EMPLOYER PROFILE: Pret a Manger at a glance." Employee Benefits, October 1, 2009, 50. http://www.proquest.com/ (30 November 2010).

Food Connections: Toward Healthy and Sustainable Food System for Toronto," *Toronto Public Health*, February 2010, http://wx.toronto.ca/inter/health/food.nsf/0dad47ac378eabca85256dcd0059fa59/E092F7D5F2C0489D852576E1006F27F3/$file/Food%20Connections%20report%20%28FINAL%29.pdf (27 November 2010).

"Food Statistics," *Statistics Canada*, 2009, http://dsp-psd.pwgsc.gc.ca/collections/collection_2010/statcan/21-020-X/21-020-x2009001-eng.pdf (27 November 2010).

"Franchising (We don't)," *Pret a Manger*, <http://www.pret.com/about/franchising.htm> (30 November 2010).

"Getting it Right: Pret A Manger", *The Insider,* August 2008, http://www-theinsider.blogspot.com/2008/08/getting-it-right-pret-manger.html (28 November 2010)

Income and Shelter Costs Metro Vancouver, *Sustainable Region Initiative* April 2009, http://www.metrovancouver.org/about/publications/Publications/Bulletin_12_final_June2009.pdf (28 November 2010).

"Introduction – SWOT Analysis of Subway", 2010 (http://www.oppapers.com/essays/Swot-Subway-Sandwich/78963 (30 November 2010)

Janet Cann (Prêt A Manger Customer Services Manager), email to author, 25 October 2010.

Kensington Natural Bakery Inc., no date, http://www.kensingtonnaturalbakery.com/index.htm (28 November 2010).

"Lessons learned from Prêt a Manger", *Restaurant Central*, no date, http://investing.businessweek.com/research/stocks/private/snapshot.asp?privcapId=685362 (28 November 2010).

"Mine's a McLatte", *The Guardian*, February 2001, http://www.guardian.co.uk/world/2001/feb/01/globalisation.foodanddrink (28 November 2010).

"Monocle: Top 25 Most Liveable Cities 2010", *Monocle Magazine*, 2010 http://www.psfk.com/2010/06/top-25-most-liveable-cities-2010.html (28 November 2010)

Organic Meadow, no date, http://www.organicmeadow.com/default.sz (28 November 2010).

"Plan B Organic Farm",*Canadian Organic Growers*, no date, http://www.cog.ca/directory/index.php?option=com_sobi2&sobi2Task=sobi2Details&catid=2&sobi2Id=2321&Itemid= (28 November 2010).

"Pret A Manger - How this successful sandwich shop filled up a gap in the market", *Startups*, March 2006, http://www.startups.co.uk/pret-a-manger.html (28 November 2010).

Prêt A Manger, no date, http://www.Prêt.com/ (26 November 2010).

Profil Socio-démographique – Agglomération de Montréal, *Montréal en statistiques*, May 2009, http://ville.montreal.qc.ca/pls/portal/docs/PAGE/MTL_STATISTIQUES_FR/MEDIA/DOCUMENTS/AGGLOM%C9RATION%20DE%20MONTR%C9AL_MAI%2009_0.PDF (28 November 2010)

"Quebec Consumers' Attitudes Towards Food Quality in Canada 2008", *Agriculture and Agri-food Canada*, November 2008 http://www4.agr.gc.ca/AAFC-AAC/display-afficher.do?id=1226523001836&lang=eng (28 November 2010)

"Recipe for Reinvention", *Fast Company*, March 2002, http://www.fastcompany.com/magazine/57/pretamanger.html (28 November 2010).

"Restaurants and Bars in the Montreal and Laval Area", *Out There*, 2004. http://www.out-there.com/tpq12_rs.htm
(28 November 2010)

"Services Sector Overview", *Industry Canada*, 2006, http://www.ic.gc.ca/eic/site/si-is.nsf/eng/ai02201.html(26 November 2010)

Shaun Smith, "Profiting From the Customer Experience Economy", pg. 5, April 2001, www.executive-conversation.pl/files/docs/Profiting_from_CEE.pdf (28 November 2010).

Stuart Smith, "How innocent are coke's reasons for taking a strategic brand stake?," *Marketing Week,* 16 April 2009, <http://www.marketingweek.co.uk/opinion/how-innocent-are-cokes-reasons-for-taking-a-strategic-brand-stake?/2065084.article> (30 November 2010).

"Success Begins With AFFINITY Resource Management," *AFFINITY Resource Management Inc.* <http://www.affinityresourcemanagement.com/> (30 November 2010).

The Charter of the French Language", *Office québecois de la langue française*, November 2010 http://www.olf.gouv.qc.ca/english/charter/title1chapter7.html (28 November 2010)

The Economy of Local Food in Vancouver, *Vancouver Economic Development Commission*, August 2009, http://www.vancouvereconomic.com/userfiles/file/Local-Food-in-Vancouver-webversion%281%29.pdf (29 November 2010).

The Healthy Butcher, no date, http://www.thehealthybutcher.com/index.html (28 November 2010).

"The State of Toronto's Food," *City of Toronto*, 2 November 2009, http://www.ryerson.ca/foodsecurity/State%20of%20Toronto%27s%20Food%20Discussion%20Paper%20%28Nov%5B1%5D.%202,%202007%29.pdf (26 November 2010).

'Toronto Competes," *City of Toronto,* http://www.toronto.ca/business_publications/tocompetes.htm#3 (27 November 2010).

"Toronto Employment Survey 2009," City of Toronto, March 2010, http://www.toronto.ca/demographics/pdf/survey2009.pdf (28 November 2010).

"Toronto Food Strategy Update," *Toronto Public Health,* 1 February 2010, http://www.toronto.ca/legdocs/mmis/2010/hl/bgrd/backgroundfile-27183.pdf (26 November 2010).

"Toronto's racial diversity," *City of* Toronto, http://www.toronto.ca/toronto_facts/diversity.htm (26 November 2010).

"Vancouver remains top, Harrare remains bottom" *Economist Intelligence Unit* 2010 http://www.eiu.com/site_info.asp?info_name=The_Global_Liveability_Report&page=noads&rf=0 (29 November 2010).

"Working for Prêt," *Prêt a Manger,* <http://www.pret.com/jobs/> (30 November 2010).

End Notes

1. "About Us" *Pret A Manger*, 2010 http://www.pret.com/about/ (29 November 2010).
2. "About Us" *Pret A Manger*, 2010 http://www.pret.com/about/ (29 November 2010).
3. "About our Company" *Pret A Manger*, 2010 http://www.pret.com/us/about_our_company/good_natural_food/ (29 November 2010).
4. „About Us" *Pret A Manger*, 2010 http://www.pret.com/about/ (29 November 2010).
5. "Lessons learned from Prêt a Manger", *Restaurant Central*, no date, http://investing.businessweek.com/research/stocks/private/snapshot.asp?privcapId=685362 (28 November 2010).
6. "Pret A Manger - How this successful sandwich shop filled up a gap in the market", *Startups*, March 2006, http://www.startups.co.uk/pret-a-manger.html (28 November 2010).
7. „Mine's a McLatte", *The Guardian*, February 2001, http://www.guardian.co.uk/world/2001/feb/01/globalisation.foodanddrink (28 November 2010).
8. „Mine's a McLatte", *The Guardian*, February 2001, http://www.guardian.co.uk/world/2001/feb/01/globalisation.foodanddrink (28 November 2010).
9. „Recipe for Reinvention", *Fast Company*, March 2002, http://www.fastcompany.com/magazine/57/pretamanger.html (28 November 2010).
10. Janet Cann (Prêt A Manger Customer Services Manager), email to author, 25 October 2010.
11. Shaun Smith, „Profiting From the Customer Experience Economy", pg. 5, April 2001, www.executive-conversation.pl/files/docs/Profiting_from_CEE.pdf (28 November 2010).
12. Shaun Smith, „Profiting From the Customer Experience Economy", pg. 5, April 2001, www.executive-conversation.pl/files/docs/Profiting_from_CEE.pdf (28 November 2010).
13. „Lessons learned from Prêt a Manger", *Restaurant Central*, no date, http://investing.businessweek.com/research/stocks/private/snapshot.asp?privcapId=685362 (28 November 2010).
14. „Getting it Right: Pret A Manger", *The Insider*, August 2008, http://www-theinsider.blogspot.com/2008/08/getting-it-right-pret-manger.html (28 November 2010)
15. „Lessons learned from Prêt a Manger", *Restaurant Central*, no date, http://investing.businessweek.com/research/stocks/private/snapshot.asp?privcapId=685362 (28 November 2010).
16. „Lessons learned from Prêt a Manger", *Restaurant Central*, no date, http://investing.businessweek.com/research/stocks/private/snapshot.asp?privcapId=685362 (28 November 2010).
17. „Pret A Manger - How this successful sandwich shop filled up a gap in the market", *Startups*, March 2006, http://www.startups.co.uk/pret-a-manger.html (28 November 2010).
18. „Pret A Manger - How this successful sandwich shop filled up a gap in the market", *Startups*, March 2006, http://www.startups.co.uk/pret-a-manger.html (28 November 2010).
19. „Lessons learned from Prêt a Manger", *Restaurant Central*, no date, http://investing.businessweek.com/research/stocks/private/snapshot.asp?privcapId=685362 (28 November 2010).
20. „Mine's a McLatte", *The Guardian*, February 2001, http://www.guardian.co.uk/world/2001/feb/01/globalisation.foodanddrink (28 November 2010).
21. „Pret A Manger (Europe) Ltd.", *Bloomberg BusinessWeek"*, November 2010, http://investing.businessweek.com/research/stocks/private/snapshot.asp?privcapId=685362 (28 November 2010).
22. Janet Cann (Prêt A Manger Customer Services Manager), email to author, 25 October 2010.
23. „Mine's a McLatte", *The Guardian*, February 2001, http://www.guardian.co.uk/world/2001/feb/01/globalisation.foodanddrink (28 November 2010).
24. „Lessons learned from Prêt a Manger", *Restaurant Central*, no date, http://investing.businessweek.com/research/stocks/private/snapshot.asp?privcapId=685362 (28 November 2010).
25. "Services Sector Overview", *Industry Canada*, 2006, http://www.ic.gc.ca/eic/site/si-is.nsf/eng/ai02201.html(26 November 2010)
26. "Canadian Food Trends to 2020", p. 25-26, *Agriculture and Agri-Food Canada Ontario*, July 2005, http://www4.agr.gc.ca/resources/prod/doc/agr/pdf/ft-ta_eng.pdf (26 November 2010).
27. "Canadian Food Trends to 2020", p. 28-29, *Agriculture and Agri-Food Canada Ontario*, July 2005, http://www4.agr.gc.ca/resources/prod/doc/agr/pdf/ft-ta_eng.pdf (26 November 2010).
28. "Canadians' Eating Habits", p. 25, *Statistics Canada*, May 2007, http://www.statcan.gc.ca/pub/82-003-x/2006004/article/habit/9609-eng.pdf (26 November 2010).
29. "Canadian Food Trends to 2020", p. 4-6, *Agriculture and Agri-Food Canada Ontario*, July 2005, http://www4.agr.gc.ca/resources/prod/doc/agr/pdf/ft-ta_eng.pdf (26 November 2010).

[30] *Prêt A Manger,* no date, http://www.Prêt.com/ (26 November 2010).

[31]"Introduction – SWOT Analysis of Subway", 2010 (http://www.oppapers.com/essays/Swot-Subway-Sandwich/78963 (30 November 2010)

[32] "Canadian Food Trends to 2020", p. 32-34, *Agriculture and Agri-Food Canada Ontario,* July 2005, http://www4.agr.gc.ca/resources/prod/doc/agr/pdf/ft-ta_eng.pdf (26 November 2010).

[33] *Prêt A Manger,* no date, http://www.Prêt.com/ (26 November 2010).

[34] „Canadian Food Trends to 2020", p. 35-36, *Agriculture and Agri-Food Canada Ontario,* July 2005, http://www4.agr.gc.ca/resources/prod/doc/agr/pdf/ft-ta_eng.pdf (26 November 2010).

[35] *Prêt A Manger,* no date, http://www.Prêt.com/ (26 November 2010).

[36] "Toronto's racial diversity," *City of* Toronto, http://www.toronto.ca/toronto_facts/diversity.htm (26 November 2010).

[37] "Toronto's racial diversity," *City of* Toronto, http://www.toronto.ca/toronto_facts/diversity.htm (26 November 2010).

[38] "Toronto's racial diversity," *City of* Toronto, http://www.toronto.ca/toronto_facts/diversity.htm (26 November 2010).

[39] "2006 Census Highlights," *Ministry of Finance,* <http://www.fin.gov.on.ca/en/economy/demographics/census/cenhi06-8.pdf> (30 November 2010).

[40] 'Toronto Competes," *City of Toronto,* http://www.toronto.ca/business_publications/tocompetes.htm#3 (27 November 2010).

[41] "The State of Toronto's Food," *City of Toronto,* 2 November 2009, http://www.ryerson.ca/foodsecurity/State%20of%20Toronto%27s%20Food%20Discussion%20Paper%20%28Nov%5B1%5D.%202,%202007%29.pdf (26 November 2010).

[42] "A Wealth of Food: A Profile of Toronto's Food Economy," *Toronto Food Policy Council,* January 1999, http://www.toronto.ca/health/tfpc_wealth.pdf (27 November 2010).

[43] Food Connections: Toward Healthy and Sustainable Food System for Toronto," *Toronto Public Health,* February 2010, http://wx.toronto.ca/inter/health/food.nsf/0dad47ac378eabca85256dcd0059fa59/E092F7D5F2C0489D852576E1006F27F3/$file/Food%20Connections%20report%20%28FINAL%29.pdf (27 November 2010).

[43] "Food Statistics," *Statistics Canada,* 2009, http://dsp-psd.pwgsc.gc.ca/collections/collection_2010/statcan/21-020-X/21-020-x2009001-eng.pdf (27 November 2010).

[44] Food Connections: Toward Healthy and Sustainable Food System for Toronto," *Toronto Public Health,* February 2010, http://wx.toronto.ca/inter/health/food.nsf/0dad47ac378eabca85256dcd0059fa59/E092F7D5F2C0489D852576E1006F27F3/$file/Food%20Connections%20report%20%28FINAL%29.pdf (27 November 2010).

[45] "The State of Toronto's Food," *City of Toronto,* 2 November 2009, http://www.ryerson.ca/foodsecurity/State%20of%20Toronto%27s%20Food%20Discussion%20Paper%20%28Nov%5B1%5D.%202,%202007%29.pdf (26 November 2010).

[46] "Average household expenditures, by selected metropolitan area – Ottawa-Gatineau, Toronto," *Statistics Canada,* 2008, http://www40.statcan.gc.ca/l01/cst01/famil10d-eng.htm (28 November 2010).

[47] "The State of Toronto's Food," *City of Toronto,* 2 November 2009, http://www.ryerson.ca/foodsecurity/State%20of%20Toronto%27s%20Food%20Discussion%20Paper%20%28Nov%5B1%5D.%202,%202007%29.pdf (26 November 2010).

[48] "Toronto Food Strategy Update," *Toronto Public Health,* 1 February 2010, http://www.toronto.ca/legdocs/mmis/2010/hl/bgrd/backgroundfile-27183.pdf (26 November 2010).

[49] "2006 Census Data on Income and Shelter Costs," *Toronto Public Health,* 1 May 2008, http://www.toronto.ca/demographics/pdf/2006_income_and_shelter_costs_briefingnote.pdf (26 November 2010).

[50] "Toronto Employment Survey 2009," City of Toronto, March 2010, http://www.toronto.ca/demographics/pdf/survey2009.pdf (28 November 2010).

[51] "Toronto Employment Survey 2009," City of Toronto, March 2010, http://www.toronto.ca/demographics/pdf/survey2009.pdf (28 November 2010).

[52] "Consumer confidence improving: Conf. Board," *CBC News,* 24 November 2010, http://www.cbc.ca/canada/toronto/story/2010/11/24/consumer-confidence-holiday-shopping.html?ref=rss (28 November 2010).

[53] "Toronto Employment Survey 2009," City of Toronto, March 2010, http://www.toronto.ca/demographics/pdf/survey2009.pdf (28 November 2010).

[54] "Toronto Employment Survey 2009," City of Toronto, March 2010, http://www.toronto.ca/demographics/pdf/survey2009.pdf (28 November 2010).

[55] "Monocle: Top 25 Most Liveable Cities 2010", *Monocle Magazine*, 2010 http://www.psfk.com/2010/06/top-25-most-liveable-cities-2010.html (28 November 2010)

[56] 2006 Census: Portrait of the Canadian Population in 2006: Subprovincial population dynamics, *Statistics Canada*, 2006, http://www12.statcan.ca/census-recensement/2006/as-sa/97-550/p14-eng.cfm (28 November 2010)

[57] 2006 Census: Portrait of the Canadian Population in 2006: Subprovincial population dynamics, *Statistics Canada*, 2006, http://www12.statcan.ca/census-recensement/2006/as-sa/97-550/p14-eng.cfm (28 November 2010)

[58] 2006 Census: Portrait of the Canadian Population in 2006: Subprovincial population dynamics, *Statistics Canada*, 2006, http://www12.statcan.ca/census-recensement/2006/as-sa/97-550/p14-eng.cfm (28 November 2010)

[59] 2006 Census: Portrait of the Canadian Population in 2006: Subprovincial population dynamics, *Statistics Canada*, 2006, http://www12.statcan.ca/census-recensement/2006/as-sa/97-550/p14-eng.cfm (28 November 2010)

[60] "The Charter of the French Language", *Office québecois de la langue française*, November 2010 http://www.olf.gouv.qc.ca/english/charter/title1chapter7.html (28 November 2010)

[61] "Restaurants and Bars in the Montreal and Laval Area", *Out There*, 2004. http://www.out-there.com/tpq12_rs.htm (28 November 2010)

[62] "Quebec Consumers' Attitudes Towards Food Quality in Canada 2008", *Agriculture and Agri-food Canada*, November 2008 http://www4.agr.gc.ca/AAFC-AAC/display-afficher.do?id=1226523001836&lang=eng (28 November 2010)

[63] "Average household expenditures, by selected metropolitan area -Québec, Montréal", *Statistics Canada*, 2008 http://www40.statcan.ca/l01/cst01/famil10c-eng.htm (28 November 2010)

[64] "About Montreal", *Mines Without Borders – CIM*, 2010 http://www.cim.org/montreal2011/registration/Montreal.cfm (28 November 2010)

[65] Profil Socio-démographique – Agglomération de Montréal, *Montréal en statistiques*, May 2009, http://ville.montreal.qc.ca/pls/portal/docs/PAGE/MTL_STATISTIQUES_FR/MEDIA/DOCUMENTS/AGGLOM%C9RATION%20DE%20MONTR%C9AL_MAI%2009_0.PDF (28 November 2010)

[66] Agri-food – General Industry Profile, *Montreal International*, 2009 http://www.montrealinternational.com/en/invest/sectors/agri-food.html (28 November 2010)

[67] About Vancouver, *City of Vancouver* 2010 http://vancouver.ca/aboutvan.htm (29 November 2010).

[68] Ibis.

[69] "Vancouver remains top, Harrare remains bottom" *Economist Intelligence Unit* 2010 http://www.eiu.com/site_info.asp?info_name=The_Global_Liveability_Report&page=noads&rf=0 (29 November 2010).

[70] Economic Profile, *Vancouver Economic Development Comission*, 2010, http://www.vancouvereconomic.com/page/economic-profile (29 November 2010).

[71] Ibis.

[72] Income and Shelter Costs Metro Vancouver, *Sustainable Region Initiative* April 2009, http://www.metrovancouver.org/about/publications/Publications/Bulletin_12_final_June2009.pdf (28 November 2010).

[73] The Economy of Local Food in Vancouver, *Vancouver Economic Development Commission*, August 2009, http://www.vancouvereconomic.com/userfiles/file/Local-Food-in-Vancouver-webversion%281%29.pdf (29 November 2010).

[74] Ibis.

[75] About Vancouver, *City of Vancouver* 2010 http://vancouver.ca/aboutvan.htm (29 November 2010).

[76] Backgrounder on the City of Vancouver Low-Income Housing Survey and Pivot Legal Society, *Pivot Legal Society*, 2005, http://intraspec.ca/Vancouver_Low-IncomeHousingSurvey2005.pdf (29 November 2010).

[77] Stuart Smith, "How innocent are coke's reasons for taking a strategic brand stake?," *Marketing Week*, 16 April 2009, <http://www.marketingweek.co.uk/opinion/how-innocent-are-cokes-reasons-for-taking-a-strategic-brand-stake?/2065084.article> (30 November 2010).

[78] "Franchising (We don't)," *Pret a Manger*, <http://www.pret.com/about/franchising.htm> (30 November 2010).

[79] 600 to 800 square feet Downtown East and Financial Core Toronto http://officesearchtoronto.com/2010/01/20/600-to-800-square-feet-dowtown-east-and-financial-core-toronto/ (30 November 2010).

[80] "Success Begins With AFFINITY Resource Management," *AFFINITY Resource Management Inc.* <http://www.affinityresourcemanagement.com/> (30 November 2010).

[81] "Working for Prêt," *Prêt a Manger,* <http://www.pret.com/jobs/> (30 November 2010).

[82] "Working for Prêt," *Prêt a Manger,* <http://www.pret.com/jobs/> (30 November 2010).

[83] "EMPLOYER PROFILE: Pret a Manger at a glance." Employee Benefits, October 1, 2009, 50. http://www.proquest.com/ (30 November 2010).

[84] "Working for Prêt," *Prêt a Manger,* <http://www.pret.com/jobs/> (30 November 2010).

[85] "Working for Prêt," *Prêt a Manger,* <http://www.pret.com/jobs/> (30 November 2010).

[86] Janet Cann (Prêt A Manger Customer Services Manager), email to author, 25 October 2010.

[87] Janet Cann (Prêt A Manger Customer Services Manager), email to author, 25 October 2010.

[88] *Prêt A Manger,* no date, http://www.Prêt.com/ (26 November 2010).

[89] *Bäckerhaus Veit,* no date, http://www.backerhausveit.com/index.php (28 November 2010).

[90] *Kensington Natural Bakery Inc.,* no date, http://www.kensingtonnaturalbakery.com/index.htm (28 November 2010).

[91] *The Healthy Butcher,* no date, http://www.thehealthybutcher.com/index.html (28 November 2010).

[92] *Organic Meadow,* no date, http://www.organicmeadow.com/default.sz (28 November 2010).

[93] „Plan B Organic Farm",*Canadian Organic Growers,* no date, http://www.cog.ca/directory/index.php?option=com_sobi2&sobi2Task=sobi2Details&catid=2&sobi2Id=2321&It emid= (28 November 2010).

[94] *Prêt A Manger,* no date, http://www.Prêt.com/ (26 November 2010).

[95] Chrissy Aitchison, "Toronto Soup Kitchens and Food Banks", 12 December 2009, http://www.blogto.com/city/2009/12/toronto_soup_kitchens_and_food_banks/ (28 November 2010).

CPSIA information can be obtained
at www.ICGtesting.com
Printed in the USA
BVHW081007130121
597713BV00007B/148